HAL•LEONARD
INSTRUMENTAL
PLAY-ALONG

CELLO

MW00667262

POPULAR HITS

HOW TO USE THE CD ACCOMPANIMENT:

A MELODY CUE APPEARS ON THE RIGHT CHANNEL ONLY. IF YOUR CD PLAYER HAS A BALANCE ADJUSTMENT, YOU CAN ADJUST THE VOLUME OF THE MELODY BY TURNING DOWN THE RIGHT CHANNEL.

THE CD IS PLAYABLE ON ANY CD PLAYER, AND IS ALSO ENHANCED SO MAC AND PC USERS CAN ADJUST THE RECORDING TO ANY TEMPO WITHOUT CHANGING THE PITCH!

ISBN 978-1-61774-005-3

HAL•LEONARD® CORPORATION

7777 W. BLUEMOUND RD. P.O. BOX 13819 MILWAUKEE, WI 53213

1 BREAKEVEN

CELLO

Words and Music by STEPHEN KIPNER, ANDREW FRAMPTON,
DANIEL O'DONOGHUE and MARK SHEEHAN

2 THE CLIMB

from HANNAH MONTANA: THE MOVIE

CELLO

Words and Music by
JESSI ALEXANDER and JON MABE

3 FALLIN' FOR YOU

CELLO

Words and Music by
COLBIE CAILLAT and RICK NOWELS

Moderate Rock

To Coda
mf
D.S. al Coda
CODA
f

4 FIREFLIES

CELLO

Words and Music by
ADAM YOUNG

5 HALO

octave tower

CELLO

Words and Music by BEYONCÉ KNOWLES, RYAN TEDDER and EVAN BOGART

HEY, SOUL SISTER

CELLO

Words and Music by PAT MONAHAN,
ESPEN LIND and AMUND BJORKLAND

1.
2.
mf
1.
2.
mf
p

7 I GOTTA FEELING

CELLO

Words and Music by WILL ADAMS,
ALLAN PINEDA, JAIME GOMEZ, STACY FERGUSON,
DAVID GUETTA and FREDERIC RIESTERER

With energy

mf
1.
2.
2

8 I'M YOURS

CELLO

Words and Music by
JASON MRAZ

Moderate Reggae (♫ = ♩♪ triplet)

2.
mf
1.
2.
f
1.
2.
2

9 LOVE STORY

CELLO

Words and Music by
TAYLOR SWIFT

mf
mp
f

10 NEED YOU NOW

CELLO

Words and Music by HILLARY SCOTT,
CHARLES KELLEY, DAVE HAYWOOD and JOSH KEAR

11 POKER FACE

CELLO

Words and Music by
STEFANI GERMANOTTA and REDONE

12 SMILE

CELLO

Words and Music by BLAIR DALY, JEREMY BOSE,
MATTHEW SHAFER and JOHN HARDING

Moderately

1.
3
2.
mf
mf
1., 2.
f
3.
2
mf

13 VIVA LA VIDA

CELLO

Words and Music by GUY BERRYMAN,
JON BUCKLAND, WILL CHAMPION and CHRIS MARTIN

Moderately

1.
3
2.
mf
1.
2.

14 YOU BELONG WITH ME

CELLO

Words and Music by
TAYLOR SWIFT and LIZ ROSE

2.
1.
2.
mp
f

15 USE SOMEBODY

CELLO

Words and Music by CALEB FOLLOWILL, NATHAN FOLLOWILL, JARED FOLLOWILL and MATTHEW FOLLOWILL